OVR LADY
✤ IN ART ✤

NIHIL OBSTAT:

Patrick J. Healy, S.T.D.,

Censor Deputatus,

Washington, D. C., May 12, 1934.

IMPRIMATUR:

✠ Michael J. Curley, D.D.,

Archiepiscopus Baltimorensis,

Baltimore, Md., May 15, 1934.

OUR LADY IN ART

✾ IN ART ✾

VOLUME I

ANNOTATIONS
AND DESCRIPTIONS BY
THE RIGHT REVEREND DAVID T. O'DWYER

PUBLISHED BY THE SALVE REGINA PRESS
THE NATIONAL SHRINE OF THE IMMACULATE CONCEPTION
WASHINGTON, D. C.

IMMACULATE CONCEPTION

Murillo (1619-1682)   *Prado, Madrid*

This great masterpiece represents some of those moments of high inspiration
which our better nature strives to make permanent; it is a sermon and a poem
on the text "Blessed are the pure of heart, for they shall see God."

4

INTRODUCTION

THE thought of Our Lady in Art is inseparable from the place she holds in history, and her influence on history is as wide as that of the Church. The conquest of the old Græco-Roman world of paganism by the Gospel, and its transmutation into the medieval world of Christianity, is the most sublime achievement of history. To recast the structure of civil society, leaving no place for the degradation of slavery; to make government a curb on despotism and the guardian of individual right; and, through justice and charity, to relieve poverty, was a consummation that pagan philosophy could not grasp, nor pagan statesmanship believe possible.

The new social order was purchased by the agonies of a long struggle which were richly rewarded by the light and joyousness the victory brought, and the rapture the new-found freedom created in the hearts of men. And the poor of Christ shared all those blessings as heirs of the kingdom which God promised to them that love Him.

When the magnificence of this new world dawned on the minds of men, they commenced, haltingly and timidly, to pour forth their tributes of praise and glorification to the Author of this gift and of all good gifts. A new note found expression in Theology, Philosophy, Poetry, Architecture, Music and Painting. All the sciences and all the arts joined in a great chorus, and from the twelfth to the fifteenth century they were blended into a triumphant crescendo of religious praise and adoration. These centuries are preeminently the period of the Catholic Middle Ages, the time when Christ ruled society, and law, and speculation, and the arts, and life itself.

Love, veneration and praise for Christ, the Son made Man, implied, also, praise for His Mother, next to the Son the chief actor in the tragedy and triumph of Redemption. With her a new vision of beauty dawned on the world. All classes in society laid their tributes at her feet. To the people she was "Our Lady", "Queen of Heaven", "Mother of God". Theo-

5

MADONNA AND CHILD

Fra Angelico (1387-1455)   *Perugia*

Fra Angelico has become for us the perfect symbol of inspired piety. Prayer
was the great preparation he made for his paintings of heavenly subjects.

logians found her prefigured in every page of the Old Testament. Poetry rang with her praises, and with Dante, deplored its insufficiency to express her perfections.

> *"I saw the Virgin smile, whose rapture shot*
> *Joy through the eyes of all that blessed throng:*
> *And even did the words that I possess*
> *Equal imagination, I should not*
> *Dare, the attempt her faintest charms to express."*

Architecture attained its highest perfection in the cathedrals and churches built in her honor, and in their adornment sculpture recaptured its ancient beauty, and in the fourteenth century painting caught the inspiration of the other two in glorifying her name. The epithet of "pagan" can have no application to the Renaissance movement that produced the works of Cimabue, Giotto and Fra Angelico. In their paintings the very soul of the Middle Ages cried out in jubilation, and so much above mere national genius are their works that they give color to the legend, related of Fra Angelico, that while he slept angels worked at his canvas in glorifying Mary. It may be that the human soul is incapable of sustained flight in a region of such mystical fervor and love as these early artists dwelt in. They worked for the glory of God, not for the glory of art, or as Ruskin has it, speaking of the time of Raphael: "In early times art was employed for the display of religious facts, now religious facts were employed for the display of art. The transition, though imperceptible, was consummate; it involved the entire destiny of painting. It passed from the paths of life to the paths of death."

It was only while religious faith and fervor governed the soul of the artist, while art was secondary to thought, that painters could transfer to canvas the lineaments of the Mary of the Middle Ages. In proportion as faith grew dim the light left their colors, and, glorious as may be the work of some of the later masters of the Renaissance, they never depicted Mary the Mother who makes intercession for all mankind.

When the Renaissance forgot the religious quality in painting, and turned frankly to the revival of a new paganism, and when the Protestant Reformation joined forces with this new paganism, art ceased to be the handmaid of religion. As Ralph Adams Cram says: "The Lutheran, Calvinist, Huguenot and Puritan agencies that grew out of the Reforma-

THE MADONNA OF CHANCELLOR ROLIN
Jan Van Eyck (1385-1440)   *Louvre, Paris*

Few names are dearer to the world of art or have more significance than the name of Van Eyck. The brothers, Hubert and Jan, were founders of the school of Bruges out of which grew all the schools of Northern Europe. In one painting they expressed the Middle Ages with perfection of sympathy and understanding, and into it, too, they introduced those elements from which all modern art has developed. Faithful historians, they also had "the prophetic soul of the wide world dreaming on things to come." The Madonna of Chancellor Rolin is only twenty-seven inches by twenty-five, and yet so marvelous is the technique that it exhibits commanding figures in a vast and varied world. The youthful Mother holds her Baby with subdued and tender pride. Her features are exquisitely delicate, and the hair which fits closely around the forehead falls in a glorious cascade over the shoulders. Her red mantle has folds whose dark shadows add subtlety to the color scheme. The kneeling Chancellor is richly garbed and has the austere melancholy of the pious man of affairs. Outside, a peaceful city reposes by a calm river flowing from blue mountains in the distance.

8

tion fell on the vast body of Christian art that inconceivably glorified all Western Europe at the end of the fifteenth century, like the hordes of Genghis Khan." Great art did not die with the triumph of Protestantism. It had a rebirth in Spain, Catholic Flanders and Italy, but the works of the later artists bear a stamp different from the pure, unearthly spirituality of the medieval period. There is a spirit in the paintings of the artists of the sixteenth and seventeenth centuries which draws and fascinates us of a later time. It may be that we, too, feel much of the nostalgic loneliness that sometimes stands revealed in their canvases.

Mary was more than a symbol of beauty to the Middle Ages: she was a force for great achievement. When Henry Adams, the American student and savant *par excellence* of the nineteenth century, visited the Paris Exposition of 1900 he was inducted by Langley into the mysteries of the dynamo. His mind went back to a visit with St. Gaudens to Amiens, and he thought of the Cathedral of Chartres, and thinking so, he said: "All the steam in the world could not, like the Virgin, build Chartres. . . . Symbol or energy, the Virgin had acted as the greatest force the Western World had ever felt, and had drawn men's activities to herself more strongly than any other power, natural or supernatural, had ever done."

Our age is tuned to the hum of the motor, the clang of the hammer, and the song of steam. Science governs our lives; but not by science alone does man live. Its advocates, like babbling children home from school and aflame with their first knowledge of the laws of nature, may affect to despise the knowledge of their elders, but the world of today has much to learn from the world in which Mary was a force superior to what the dynamo or the motor can ever become. It is in the hope that the world may again come back to thoughts of Mary that we are publishing these pictures in which she appears as she was seen through the eyes of faith in centuries long gone by. She was a force for great things then: she may be so again if we so desire.

DAVID T. O'DWYER.

9

MADONNA AND CHILD

Fra Filippo Lippi (1406-1469)   *Pitti, Florence*

Though the most tolerant critic must admit that Fra Lippi deserved serious
moral censure, his lapses have been exaggerated, and the circumstances
which modify his guilt have not been given due consideration. His age was
far from strict, and his genius and the patronage of him by the Medici offered
him a tempting immunity. Pope Pius II dispensed him from his vows, after
which he married Lucretia Buti, who had been the object of his illicit passion.

It was Filippo Lippi's distinction not merely to paint great pictures, but to
become one of the great formative influences in the evolution of the art of his
time. Like Edmund, in King Lear, nature was his goddess, but he had
Wordsworth's spiritual perception, and he could see the significance of the
meanest flower that blows. No man ever saw the beauty of nature with a
more sympathetic eye; and nobody ever conveyed it more faithfully. Lucretia
Buti posed for this Madonna, which is supposed to be her most faithful likeness.
She is not quite equal to her rôle, and her face has none of the transfiguration
of divine maternity. The Child has a look of tender appeal, and the coming
events of sorrow have cast their shadows on His face.

In the background the meeting of Joachim and Anne, and the birth of the
    Blessed Virgin, are represented in scenes of tender, imaginative feeling.

10

VIRGIN, CHILD AND ST. JOHN

Fra Filippo Lippi (1406-1469)   *Staatlich Museum, Berlin*

Lippi's art expresses the harmoniously blent influences of two masters. A strength and a solidity belonging to the earth on which we live, are the result of Masaccio's teaching; and a consecration of them, to express the heaven which is our destiny, is the secret he learnt from Fra Angelico. But the influences he absorbed did not impair his individuality. He was always himself. He was the first great artist to make his religious figures perfectly human. No figure was so etherealised that we could not feel some kinship with it. His Madonnas were real women and "not too good for human nature's daily food". This Virgin, though redolent of her great prerogatives, still has a sweet humanity to which we feel akin. Her downcast eyes and parted lips tell that she gazes on more than a mere baby, and her hands express a motion of ecstatic gratitude. The diaphanous drapery of her head and the sculptural grace with which her robes fall are superb. The Father and Holy Ghost are expressed symbolically, and the splendor of Their setting and the light They shed on the scene indicate the ineffable condescension of the Incarnation.

11

THE SISTINE MADONNA (*Detail*)

Raphael Santi (1483-1520)   *Dresden*

This Madonna is the "Lady with the Veil" elevated to a spirituality which art has never excelled. A contemplation of her face, particularly of her eyes which have looked on things not given to man to utter, creates in us that trance in which we listen to ravishing music. The enchantment of her heavenly vision has been imparted to her garments and her shawl swells majestically as though with a breeze from paradise. The Child is held with the perfection of ease and grace. He is not the child who thinks as a child; the mature seriousness of the mouth, the intense earnestness of the eyes and the disordered condition of the hair indicate pre-occupation with the stupendous work of man's redemption.

12

MADONNA ENTHRONED WITH ANGELS AND SAINTS
Matteo di Giovanni di Bartolo (1420-1495)   Church of S. Maria, Siena
The Virgin of Discretion holds in her lap the Child of Wisdom Who blesses
two kneeling mortals while angelic choirs offer celestial fruits above.

13

MADONNA AND CHILD *(Detail)*

Hans Memling (1430-1494)   *Staatlich Museum, Berlin*

Memling, a German expatriate, became one of the great glories of the Flemish
School, whose technique he mastered and enriched with a poetic conception
that rescued Flemish art from the bleak commonplaceness to which, in its very
perfection, it tended. His Madonna has the dignity and grace of a queen; and
the Infant is unquestionably of the blood royal. The Second Eve gives the
fruit to the Second Adam, who seems to ponder on what his acceptance
involves for ransoming the fallen race.

14

MADONNA WITH CHILD AND ANGELS

Hans Memling (1430-1494)   *Uffizi, Florence*

Wealth of imagination and delicate poetic feeling characterize this picture.
The grouping of the figures is superb. The highly decorative setting harmonizes
with the dignity of the personages, and the imposing background, with castle
and cottage, shows the comprehensive mercy of the Incarnation, which is
extended to both rich and poor.

MADONNA AND SAINTS

Bartolommeo Vivarini (c1430-c1499)   *Museum, Naples*

Three of the Vivarini family attained distinction in art and contributed to the glory of the Venetian School. Bartolommeo was the younger brother of Antonio, whose son, Alvise, owed much to the training of his uncle. Notwithstanding the proximity of Venice to Florence, the School of Florence started some one hundred and fifty years before the School of Venice. But when the latter did arise, it was marked by a superb richness that attested the opulence of the city of the Doges. This picture has excellent composition and extraordinary richness of detail, and it is resplendent with the golden glow of Venetian painting. The slumbering infant is tenderly human but the rapt adoration of the Madonna and the spellbound reverence of the surrounding figures unveil the divinity that helpless humanity conceals. Vivarini combined sculpture with painting, which a statuesque quality in the figures recalls.

16

MADONNA AND CHILD

Carlo Crivelli (1430-1493)   *Brera, Milan*

The paintings of Crivelli are almost the sole record he has left. He liked to put stately figures in a setting, highly decorative, and rich in architectural detail. Fruit and flower, crown and throne, and rich drapery give the Madonna and Child the homage of art and nature.

17

MADONNA AND CHILD

Domenico Ghirlandaio (1449-1494)   *Uffizi, Florence*

Ghirlandaio is the joyous painter of an untroubled world. Life did not present him with many perplexities; and his paintings have a serenity that expresses his perfect content. He began life as a goldsmith—his name indicates that calling—and his Madonna and Child shows how effectively he made use of his early training. The jewels are lavish though they do not offend. He is seen at his best in his portraits. He will always be remembered as the teacher of Michelangelo, but he has a claim on posterity for his example as well as for his precept.

18

ADORATION OF THE MAGI

Domenico Ghirlandaio (1449-1494)   *Foundling Hospital, Flor.*

Ghirlandaio studied the great masters to advantage and, if his paintings record his impressions without much originality, they have undeniable charm. The figures in this picture have ease, grace and animation. The reverent humility with which the Infant's foot is adored is most impressive. Even the animals are subdued to harmony with the worshipful scene. The Madonna is a study of quiet rapture. The opulent touches of the background should make visitors from the gorgeous East feel at home.

MADONNA OF THE MAGNIFICAT

Alessandro Botticelli (1447-1510)   *Uffizi, Florence*

The appeal of Botticelli is indefinable. He does not grip you with the convulsive interest of Michelangelo; nor does he enchant you with the serene loveliness of Raphael; but he both agitates and soothes you in a way that is unique. His pictures impress you, first of all, with intensity of feeling and poetic conception. The circle is balanced with flawless perfection. In the background to the right of the Madonna you glimpse the graceful windings of a stream through rich meadowland whose flatness is relieved by trees. Two angels, with hands of captivating beauty of line, hold over the head of the Madonna a golden crown of exquisite tracery. The angel on the right has an entrancing look of boyish innocence. Beside the Madonna's knee, two angels stand; and the one who holds the inkwell has a gentle eagerness to serve the Handmaid of the Lord. His companion gazes into his face with joyous earnestness. The angel behind them completes the circle and calls attention to the main interest of the picture. The book in which the Madonna is about to write has some of the text of her Magnificat. Her Son lays His right hand on her wrist as if to guide her writing; His left hand grasps the bitten fruit, symbol of the cause of all our woe. He looks toward heaven and His parted lips seem to breathe His Mother's Magnificat.

MADONNA AND CHILD WITH SEVEN ANGELS

Alessandro Botticelli (1117-1510)   Kaiser Frederich Museum, Berlin

Possibly, no artist gave such earnest and sympathetic study to the Madonna
as Botticelli. Fra Lippi taught him the technique to express his religious
feeling. Dante, for whose poems he furnished such marvelous illustrations,
showed him that sound theology and faithful adherence to Christian tradition can be clothed in matchless art; and through Savonarola's preaching, he
received poignant and elevating inspiration to portray the sorrows of Christ's
stricken Mother.

In this picture, the Madonna stands, full length, before a niched throne. It is
no sudden grief that pierces us in that sad face, for it has the languor of
habitual mournful contemplation. The Baby, standing on the richly carved
arm of a chair, leans slightly against His Mother, and His left hand gently lays
hold of her dress where it is open at the neck; His right is extended in blessing.
His face shows the mysterious seriousness of infancy and the gentleness of
divine compassion. The excellence of Botticelli's lineal design was never surpassed by a European. It is only the East, with its much longer artistic history,
that can show anything like Botticelli's perfection in line. The fall of the
angelic drapery and the turn of their heads no artist ever excelled.

21

MADONNA AND ANGELS

Alessandro Botticelli (1447-1510)   *Palazzo Corsini, Florence*

This picture, one of the most precious heirlooms of the Corsini family, came
into their possession towards the end of the Seventeenth Century. Six angels
surround the Madonna and Child. The pose of the Child standing astride
His Mother's knees is unusual. He is tense with an activity impossible in a
seating posture, and His eyes search His Mother's face with stricken inquiry.
She has the forebodings of great sorrow. The vivid and thoughtful angels reg-
ister every feeling from sadness to dismay. The picture gives a general impression of tragic crisis, which is borne out by an examination of its elements. Two
angels hold over the Virgin's head a crown, stuck with branches of lily palm
and olive, and at the same time they draw back the curtains of a baldaquin.
In front of them and on the left side of the picture, one angel holds the spear
and another the sponge; on the right side one angel holds the crown of thorns
and another the nails. All the figures seem to emerge from the curtains as if
the veil of the future were lifting, and the prophecy of Simeon's piercing sword
being disclosed. The left hand of the Madonna has a gesture of reassuring
endearment. The Child listens and surmises, and His lips open with an
expression of divine compassion as if He desired the chalice to pass from her.

22

MADONNA AND SAINTS

Andrea de Verrocchio (1435-1488)   *Uffizi, Florence*

Though Verrocchio was more renowned as sculptor than painter, the teacher
of Leonardo, di Credi, and Perugino, must always engage the serious attention
of students of painting. He was the friend of Lorenzo de Medici, for whom he
executed commissions, but he lacked the desire of profiting by association with
the rich and munificent, and his worldly fortunes did not exceed the humble
competence that was the ideal of Solomon. He lived with a married sister who
was blessed with many children, and they apparently supplied all the happiness of family life he desired, for he never married. And that his celibacy was
neither selfish nor cynical is proved by the fact that he excelled in depicting
the innocent charm of children and the appealing beauty of womanly grace.
In this picture, a Madonna of delicate refinement sits superbly enthroned, hold-
ing an Infant Who seems to shrink from the tragedy which St. Francis contemplates in the crucifix. St. Nicholas of Bari, kneeling, offers gifts depicting
the wealth and learning of the world; and the standing St. Zenobius presents
the model of a cathedral which symbolizes the seat of the authority in Christ's
Church. The Baptist holds the scroll which promises the forgiveness of Sin.

23

MADONNA AND CHILD

Giovanni Santi (1435-1494)   *Nat. Gal., London*

Santi was the father of Raphael, and though he died before his son was old
enough to be moulded by his artistic influence, it is not altogether fanciful
to say we discover a family resemblance in the paintings of father and son.
The Child is asleep with the sweet, untroubled weariness of infancy. The
Divine Mother seems to hold her breath lest she disturb Him. In her face is
a marvelous blend of divine adoration and human solicitude. Inanimate
nature in the background is radiant with perfect serenity as if the peace of
her slumbering God had descended upon her.

24

MADONNA AND CHILD WITH TWO SAINTS
Pietro Perugino (c1446-1524)   *Uffizi, Florence*

Perugino, the founder of the Umbrian School, the associate of Leonardo, and the teacher of Raphael, has many titles to fame. He was a man of both genius and indefatigable industry. Unfortunately, no work of his prior to 1482 survives, and three of his frescoes had to submit to the ignominy of destruction to give place to the more resplendent creations of Michelangelo's Last Judgment. He was much in demand as a painter of religious pictures, and his frescoes and altar pieces adorned the churches of many cities. He is recognized as the originator of the "pious picture," that is, he was the first to set out, with obvious intent, to edify by painting. This picture shows distinguished mastery of anatomy. Saint Sebastian's upward gaze discovers a solace that makes him indifferent to the arrows that pierce him, and the Madonna looks in his direction as if mindful of Simeon's prophecy of her own transfixion. The "Child is father of the Man" of Sorrows, and the Baptist ponders with the mournful gravity of high tragedy.

MADONNA WITH CHRIST CHILD AND ST. JOHN

Lorenzo di Credi (1459-1537)   *Borghese Gal., Rome*

Di Credi was that rare thing, a docile genius. The great influences of his
life were mirrored in his work, and yet his individuality was not impaired.
The zeal of Savonarola, whose ardent disciple he was, speaks through his
paintings in accents attuned to his own gentle nature. His great friend, the
incomparable Leonardo, with whom he studied under Verrocchio, embodied
the artistic perfection at which he aimed, an effort rewarded by something
more than the accuracy of imitation. The face of the Madonna has a light of
gentle peace and sweet maternal concern. The embrace of her left arm
brings the Baptist into that intimate association with her Divine Son which
was part of the novitiate that prepared the precursor for the rôle he played
with such heroic loyalty.

The attire of the Madonna is queenly, and the rigidity of its folds and the firm
yet delicate waves of her hair show the young goldsmith surviving in the mature painter. The pose of the Madonna's head and the grouping of the figures
are the secret he learnt from Leonardo, but the spirit that animates these
figures is his own.

26

ADORATION OF THE CHILD JESUS

Lorenzo di Credi (1459-1537)   *Uffizi, Florence*

Di Credi was one of those artists whom the spell of Savonarola inspired to paint for the greater honor and glory of God; his "Adoration of the Child Jesus" is a "Venite Adoremus" (Come, Let Us Adore) for all who gaze on it. The graceful inflexibility of the Madonna's drapery recalls the artist's early apprenticeship to a goldsmith. The pose of her head is exquisitely devotional; the eyes are so veiled that they can contemplate only one object; the mouth has an expression of brooding gratitude; and the hands show their ministerial consecration to the needs of the Divine Child. The Divine Infant has all the tenderness and sweetness of babyhood, and yet, through the garment of His humanity, the radiance and power of the divinity appear. His countenance at once acknowledges and justifies the worship He receives. We cannot feel that it is mere physical weariness which overcomes St. Joseph. The mystery of God's dealings with men, the bewilderment of his humility over the astounding prerogative which Providence bestowed on him, are expressed in that mystified tranquillity which reposes on the aging face. The grouping has the artistic perfection of Leonardo, with whom Di Credi studied under Verrocchio. The solid masonry against which Our Lady is posed and the landscape in the distance suggest Leonardo's "Virgin of the Rocks."

27

MADONNA IN THE MEADOW

Raphael Santi (1483-1520)   *Vienna*

The excellence of this picture is the reward of much patient study. Many pre-
liminary drawings of it exist, and we know that Raphael studied with Fra
Bartolommeo the problem of triangular grouping of which this picture is such
a triumphant solution. Fra Bartolommeo never passed a certain stiff formality
in his efforts, whereas the younger artist attained perfect naturalness. Leonardo's influence is shown in the color scheme, the feminine grace of the
Madonna, and in the treatment of the landscape. The Madonna shows the
marks of exquisite breeding. Her shoulders have rare beauty of contour and
her hands are excellently drawn. The feet of her Child are posed in a faltering
step and she supports His advance toward the kneeling St. John to whom He
presents the cross.

MADONNA OF FOLIGNO

Raphael Santi (1483-1520)   *Vatican, Rome*

Pope Julius gave Raphael permission to paint this picture for his Chamberlain, Sigismond Conti, in thanksgiving for his escape from a bomb during the siege of his city, Foligno, seen in the distance. The Madonna and Child are enthroned in the clouds and are lovingly contemplated by playful cherubs.

MADONNA OF THE GOLDFINCH

Raphael Santi (1483-1520)   *Uffizi, Florence*

A unique joyousness characterizes this Madonna. She has been reading to her Son, Who, still gravely attentive, turns to St. John, who is tense with excitement over his capture of the Goldfinch. The Divine Child does not resent the interruption; and lays His hand on the bird's head to encourage the young bird lover. The landscape is exquisitely beautiful and the fern-like trees, perfectly still, wait for the bird to sing from their branches the Te Deum of his coming release.

MADONNA OF THE CHAIR

Raphael Santi (1483-1520)   *Pitti, Florence*

"The Madonna of the Chair" is the most popular of all Raphael's paintings.
It was painted toward the end of his career, and illustrates the maturity of his
genius. The closeness of the three heads indicates sympathetic relationship.
The chair gives a domestic touch, and we feel that St. Joseph is near. The
Divine Child seems startled or frightened, but His Mother's arms are a refuge
and a protection. His fears are not yet allayed and His eyes and left hand tell
of lingering disquiet. St. John is just a little bit remote as if his humility holds
him back, but the radiance of his countenance shows association with the
Divine Child. The head of the Madonna is exquisitely moulded and her face
has a modesty that borders on shyness. She is the contadina, or peasant type,
and is arrayed in colors that are extraordinarily rich; but the delicate harmony
of light and shade prevents garishness. St. John's cross is a foreshadow of
Calvary in the peaceful home at Nazareth.

31

THE VIRGIN OF THE ROCKS

Leonardo da Vinci (1452-1519)   *Nat. Gal., London*

Leonardo was possibly the most versatile genius of all time. He departed
from classical tradition and became a classic himself. The Virgin of the
Rocks has power and delicacy; the strength and tenderness of nature are
there; and an artistic grouping of figures unexcelled in painting.

HEAD OF THE VIRGIN (*Detail*)

Pieter Claeyssens, the Elder (1500-1576)   *Louvre, Paris*

Pieter Claeyssens was a member of a Bruges family, prolific in painters. He
entered the Guild of St. Luke in his native city in 1516, became a Master in
1529, and Dean in 1572. He was a painter of history and portraits. This picture represents the Virgin without the Child, but at every stroke of the brush
the painter was mindful of Him. We look at the Virgin's face and ask "how
such a glance came there?" Calvary and the Stabat Mater contain the answer.

THE BURGOMASTER MEYER MADONNA

Hans Holbein, the Younger (1497-1543)   *Darmstadt Gallery*

Holbein and Dürer are the commanding figures in German art. Holbein did
not have the versatility of other great masters such as Van Dyck and Titian,
but as a portrait painter he surpassed them.

THE ALBERETTI MADONNA

Giovanni Bellini (1430-1516)   *Accademia Di Belle Arti, Venice*

Giovanni Bellini owed much to the artistic instruction and example of his
father, Giacomo, and his brother, Gentile, both of whom he surpassed. He
and Gentile were the chief founders of the Venetian School. The interest
of a new technique in painting stimulated the budding genius of Giovanni
to become its most distinguished exponent. He attained his highest
excellence in devotional pictures which show much genuine spiritual insight.
The face of his Madonna is painted with rich and reverent imagination, and
her drapery is a wonder of artistic arrangement. She holds, with worshiping
tenderness, an Infant Who is truly the Lamb of God.

35

VIRGIN AND CHILD (*Detail*)

Murillo (1619-1682)   *Pitti, Florence*

The soul of Spain, in its devotion to the Blessed Virgin, is reflected in the
Madonnas of Murillo. A note of rapturous anguish runs through them.

THE VIRGIN WITH CHILD

Albrecht Dürer (1471-1528)   *Hof Museum, Vienna*

Dürer, goldsmith, engraver, painter, man of scholarly tastes and attainments, with a knowledge of the art of antiquity, Italy, and the Netherlands, was, nevertheless, German of the Germans, and in everything he did, his race and his people spoke. He left his beloved Nuremberg only three times in his life, and the city is still redolent of the great artist's passionate love. His Madonna has rare depth of feeling, a certain cloistral simplicity, and the dignity of deep modesty. The Infant is the lovely Child of such a Mother, but His eyes see further than the eyes of a Child; through them shines the undying love of God for men.

MADONNA AND CHILD

Luini (1470-1533)   *Collection of Sir Austen Layard, Venice*

Practically no details of Luini's life are available, but his work remains and
excites an interest born of unquestionable merit and also of their resemblance
to Leonardo's work. No Italian painter shows the influence of Leonardo to
such a marked degree. What was strongest in Leonardo is not reproduced,
and his entrancing fascination is lacking, but Leonardo, in his gentler moods
and in his rare skill in chiaroscuro, is there. Luini's Madonna has a surpassing
sweetness of expression which does not cloy by reason of the light of a searching intelligence and dawning wonder which illumines her face. The Infant
has strength and vigor and is a splendid early study of Christ the King.

38

MADONNA OF THE ROSE BOWER

Luini (1470-1533)   *Brera, Milan*

So little is known of Luini that we have to look for his life in his paintings. The quest is an inviting one, for his work shows fine technique in which the influence of Leonardo is evident. His paintings, however, reveal a certain sweetness and devotion which were lacking in his master. The Madonna of the Rose Bower is his best work. Its decorative features are highly attractive. The roses, in their various stages of unfolding, have the life of growing things, and one feels that they add fragrance as well as beauty to the scene. The Virgin is truly an adoring mother, and a certain masterfulness appears in the Child, the development of which led to the great scene in which the money changers were driven from the temple.

MADONNA AND CHILD

Cima da Conegliano (1460-1517)   *Bologna Gallery*

Cima is one of the glories of the Venetian School. He owed much to Alvise
and Bartolommeo Montagna, but his highest inspiration came from Giovanni
Bellini. He marks a stage in the development beginning with Bellini and
reaching consummation in Titian. His reminiscences of the one have the
stamp of his own personality, and his anticipations of the other, the promising
dawn of a fuller day. He was one of the first to make landscape a setting for
his figures, and this picture effectively disposes mountains, river, trees, and
buildings. Nature here presents something of a stern aspect, and the crag to
the left has a bold assertiveness. Against the frowning majesty of this background, the figures display unruffled repose. The Madonna has thoughtful
dignity and is draped with graceful and chaste elegance. She tenderly sustains
the standing Child, Whose full eyes and parted lips express a naïve wonder.

HOLY FAMILY

Luca Signorelli (1441-1523)   *Uffizi, Florence*

Signorelli achieved distinction as a creative artist, and his influence was strongly felt in the development of the art of his time. He was also a man of affairs with weight in the counsels of his government and was at various times intrusted with important administrative office. He contributed something new to the technique of composition. His figures show that power and movement which afterwards Michelangelo developed to the point of violence. He had both vigor of conception and mastery in execution, and in no appraisal of Renaissance art can his work be ignored. The figures in his Holy Family are very clearly differentiated. St. Joseph has a masculine strength and a muscular power for which sculpture rather than painting is the medium. The figure gives the impression of towering, and it awes rather than pleases. Our Lady is sweetly maternal and turns over the pages of the book to the accompaniment of ineffable thoughts and emotions. The Child has the precocious wisdom which astounded the doctors in the temple, and the authority which declared, "It was said to them of old . . . but I say to you." The book which Our Lady holds plays an important part in the composition. It is in the center of the picture; it is the object of St. Joseph's reverent contemplation, and suggests thoughts to the wondering Child.

41

MADONNA AND CHILD

Paolo Morando (1486-1522)　　　　　　　　*National Gallery, London*

Notwithstanding the fact that Verona has many frescoes and paintings by
Morando and that two of his paintings hang in the National Gallery in London,
encyclopedias, including the Catholic, fail to mention him. Bryan's Dictionary
is the only source of information concerning him in the Library of Congress.

This picture shows John the Baptist presenting a fruit to the Divine Child, for
which He reaches with gentle eagerness. He is held by the Madonna with
pensive tenderness; and an angel behind her contemplates the scene with
characteristic wonder and awe. The faces have the curving delicacy and grace
of the Venetian School. Saint John has the rich lustrous eyes of the Italian;
and the Divine Infant has that pathetic tenderness which makes us anticipate,
with a pang, the tragedy that awaits Him. The delicate oval face of the
Madonna is well drawn; and the marvelous coloring of the Venetian School
gives the entire composition dignity and splendor.

MADONNA OF THE HARPIES

Andrea del Sarto (1487-1531)   *Uffizi, Florence*

Del Sarto was an artist who has been denied his meed of due recognition. A world, intoxicated with the greater genius of Michelangelo, Leonardo, and Raphael, with whom it has been his fate always to be contrasted, failed to appreciate his milder wine. Charges of shiftlessness and dishonesty in money matters have not been sustained by later research, and a marriage, to which gossip has been neither generous nor just, created an impression of ineffectualness in the man which was read into his works. But it was not the legendary Del Sarto who was strong enough to withstand the fastidiousness of a taste that would be satisfied with nothing less than Michelangelo, Leonardo, and Raphael, and who in the face of adverse fashion upheld his own individuality. The charm of his "soft silver harmonies" will soothe hearts weary of the harshness of life and his superb coloring give them stimulation.

43

VIRGIN ADORING (*Detail*)

Fra Filippo Lippi (1406-1469)   *Uffizi, Florence*

The disciples, having seen Our Lord in prayer, one of them begged: "Lord, teach us to pray." A study of Lippi's "Virgin Adoring" inspires us to make the same request. The whole figure, even the drapery, breathes attraction to the divine. She has a brow of serene contemplation. Candor and innocence are in her face. Her eyes behold an entrancing vision and her lips, delicate, yet firm, express the resolve to carry out its promptings. Her hands are clasped in an ecstasy of surrender to God's service.

44

MADONNA AND SAINTS

Francesco de Bianchi (Il Frari) (1447-1510)   *Louvre, Paris*

Bianchi's association with the boy Correggio has led to some speculation as to
his influence on the greater artist's career. A Madonna of graceful simplicity
and a Child of winning charm are the subjects of the austere meditation of
Saint Bernard and the chivalrous devotion of Saint Quentin.

45

MADONNA AND CHILD

Giovanni Sogliani (1492-1544)   *Uffizi, Florence*

Few men of genius or talent could have had a career more favorable to their development than Sogliani. He was a pupil of Lorenzo di Credi with whom he worked over twenty years. Thus he had apprenticeship and collaboration with an artist who took great pains with his work, and with a man associated with the greatest artists of his age—the pupil of Verrocchio, the confrere and friend of Perugino and Leonardo. Sogliani, therefore, had rare opportunities to develop industry and receive inspiration. His work has the evidence of his master's spirit and technique, but he was not merely the steadfast votary of one shrine. He saw in Fra Bartolommeo much that he strove to make his own. He was engaged with Del Sarto in decorating the Pisan Duomo, and some of the graces of that gentle artist reappear in Sogliani.

MADONNA AND SAINTS

Palma Vecchio (1480-1523)   *S. Stefano, Vicenza*

Palma had high gifts as a portrait painter, both of men and women, but he
depicted women with a keener and more sympathetic understanding.

47

MADONNA DI S. GIROLAMO

Correggio (1494-1534)   *Parma*

The mystery of genius was never more strikingly illustrated than in Correggio,
who had no teachers, and who did not visit famous art centers, and who,
nevertheless, became one of the great Italian masters to whom the secret of
every technical device in painting was revealed. This picture shows his skill
in perspective and the strength and tenderness of his religious emotion. The
light of Christ illumines all the figures, and their various ages show how all
sufficing He is for human needs.

VIRGIN IN ADORATION

Correggio (1494-1534)   *Uffizi, Florence*

We know little of Correggio's life; but his paintings make us feel that he had moments of great happiness and on the whole a large measure of content, and that whatever sorrow came his way deepened his sympathetic nature.

His Virgin adores with no memory of sin to give her anguish, and with such surrender of love as shuts out any fear of the grief the years might bring. Her hands express a rapture of helpless ecstasy. The Incarnation never seemed more condescending than in that Tiny Form, Whose radiance transfigures her. "A privacy of glorious light is hers," and as we gaze, the intrusion seems pardoned by those stirrings which help us to grope towards the supernatural.

MADONNA ENTHRONED

Fra Bartolommeo (1475-1517)   *Prado, Madrid*

Fra Bartolommeo is famous for his paintings, for his influence on Raphael,
and for the transformation wrought on his character and work by Savonarola.
He is part of that mounting wave which brought Renaissance art to its highest
splendor. Bartolommeo's Madonna, with gentle rapture, holds a resolute and
radiant Infant. St. Anne dramatically appeals to heaven which gave the glory
in which she played a part.

MADONNA AND SAINTS

Da Imola (1494-1550)   *R. Pinacoteca, Bologna*

Da Imola had delicate sensibility and rare skill in craftsmanship but lacked
creative genius. He was eleven years younger than Raphael and survived
him thirty years; but he was so dominated during his entire career by the
genius of the greater artist that his work is too imitative to give the highest
artistic pleasure. As one studies his paintings, one is led to speculate whether
if Raphael had not lived Da Imola would have been an artist at all, or a very
much greater one than he was. The fascinating tenderness of the children,
the pensive dignity of the Madonna, the love of St. Francis and the fervor
of St. Catherine, make the picture one of rare emotional appeal.

ADORATION UNDER THE BALDACCHINO
Alessandro Botticelli (1446-1510)   *Ambrosiana, Milan*

The background of this picture was suggested by the hills outside Florence
overlooking the Arno. The central figures are in a sumptuous pavilion whose
rich curtains are drawn back by two angels, whose action, while disclosing the
outside world, leaves the Mother and her Baby and attendant angel in sacred
privacy. An angel helps the uncertain steps of the Child as He seeks His
exuberant Mother, who kneels to Him and with enticing gesture prepares to
satisfy His needs. Below in the foreground is a vase of lilies, and the opening
made by the curtains is crowned by a wreath of rich foliage. The fluttering
draperies of the angels fall with that felicity in which no one excelled Botticelli.
The variety and harmony of the colors show him at his best. The purple
dress and azure mantle of the Madonna make an effective and characteristic
contrast. The face and bearing of the supporting angel display an adoring
solicitude. The angel on the left wears a pale saffron dress, whose tints
contrast effectively with the rich purple curtain bordered with pearls and
gold. The clear and tranquil light of the landscape tempers the resplendent
colors of the heavenly figures to the capacity of mere mortal eyes and induces
the mood of a serene spiritual contemplation.

MADONNA AND CHILD

Il Sodoma (1477-1549)   *Brera, Milan*

Il Sodoma, the friend of Raphael and the pupil of Leonardo, was a genius of
many gifts, which very often failed of adequate expression through apathy
or indolence. His Madonna has a shy and tender grace and a rare delicacy
of feminine charm. The Divine Child has an affectionate playfulness to
which in other portraits of children by the artist is added an engaging mis-
chievousness. His caressing of the lamb is a symbol of the love with which
He redeemed the world. But the lamb, while being symbolical, also adds to
the emotionalism of the painting and thus harmonizes with the face of the
Mother and Child. The Madonna is gently reminiscent of the Mona Lisa,
but the fascination of the enigmatic smile is lacking. The landscape is well
treated. The tall tree with its delicate tracery stands frail against a menacing
sky, and an atmosphere of slumbering warmth envelops the whole.

53

MADONNA OF THE PESARO FAMILY

Titian (1477-1576)   *Church of the Frari, Venice*

Titian, the greatest of Venetian painters, achieved such distinction in the
handling of color that his name has become part of its vocabulary. He had
superb skill in light and shade, and with a few strokes of the brush could
achieve almost miraculous characterization.

MADONNA AND CHILD WITH ST. ANNE
Girolamo dai Libri (1474-1556)   *Nat. Gal., London*

Artists in their rare introduction of St. Anne in pictures of the Holy Family give her a prominence denied the father and spouse of the Virgin. Her sustaining arm insists that *her daughter* is the Mother of God. A radiant Infant takes up the chant of the angels, but the Mothers do not catch the note of joy.

55

HOLY FAMILY

Peter Paul Rubens (1575-1640)   *Pitti, Florence*

Rubens is the most prolific of the masters. His imagination was so rich and triumphant that a large collection of his paintings, such as you see in the Louvre, gives an impression of overwhelming splendor. His religious pictures have a depth of fervor and intensity attributable to the special solicitude with which his Catholic mother trained him in a faith unshared by his father. His greatest painting is the Descent from the Cross, which hangs in the Cathedral at Antwerp. His Holy Family is a marvel of delineation. The Divine Child, so lovable and tender, gazes with kindly yet searching interest on the shyly caressing child who seems eager to play with Him. The Madonna restrains her ecstasy, and the other figures have a joyous yet reverent awareness of a Great Presence.

HOLY FAMILY

Bonifazio Veneziano (16th Century)   Church of San Pietro, near Perugia

Bonifazio was a pupil of Palma Vecchio who strove, with unabashed zeal, to imitate the great master, Titian. In this he was so successful that some doubtful Titians are attributed to him and *vice versa*. Bonifazio had many gifts of a high order, but in their production he lacked something which defeated their promise. He had an excellent color sense which failed to achieve corresponding beauty of treatment. He had a grace of composition which was not wedded to worthy conceptions, and his execution had an ease and inevitableness adequate to nobler designs, all of which makes us exclaim, "Oh! the little more, and how much it is; and the little less, and what worlds away." At the moment his skill was applied, the fire of his imagination seemed to cool, and genuine warmth of soul failed to enliven his subject. This picture illustrates both the excellence and limitations of the artist.

MADONNA AND SAINTS

Anthony Van Dyck (1599-1641)   *Lucca*

Van Dyck was one of the greatest portrait painters that ever lived. This picture shows those qualities that arrest and enthrall in his portraits of nobility and royalty. The heads are poised with the perfection of ease and dignity. The Divine Child is a most ethereal conception of the Incarnation, and His Mother shows the "great things done for her." The burning ardor of St. Francis explains the stigmata he bears; and the kneeling prelate is lost in the wonder of rapturous adoration. The artist's familiarity with the kingly court is shown in the deliberate postures, which are formal without being stiff.

58

MADONNA AND CHILD

Murillo (1619-1682)   *Corsini Gallery, Rome*

Bartolome Murillo was almost exclusively a painter of religious subjects. He had a gentle and affectionate nature which expressed itself in all his works. The sorrows of the gospel made a constant appeal to him, and he portrayed it with tender pity. His Blessed Virgin is literally full of grace.

MADONNA OF THE GRAND DUKE

Raphael Santi (1483-1520)   *Pitti, Florence*

Grand Duke Ferdinand, for whom this picture was named, so loved it that he
carried it with him everywhere he went.

THE MADONNA

Carlo Dolci (1616-1686)   *Uffizi, Florence*

Dolci was a master who won the enthusiastic recognition of his contemporaries. Their approval posterity has sustained. The form which his predecessors in the Renaissance developed, he enriched with many emotional qualities, using chiaroscuro with extraordinary skill. His piety was so absorbing that his art only responded to religion. But the austere did not appeal to him, and his faces express only soft, gentle and tender emotions. His Madonna is not tragic; but in the beautifully illuminated face we find a touching sadness which the dark, surrounding draperies enfold with sorrow.

61

LIST OF ILLUSTRATIONS

ACKNOWLEDGMENT

My thanks are due to Mr. Frederick V. Murphy, Head of the Department of Architecture of The Catholic University of America, for many valuable suggestions in the preparation of this volume, and to Dr. Leicester B. Holland, Chief of the Division of Fine Arts, Library of Congress, and his assistant, Mr. David E. Roberts, for aid in the study of the Bolton Collection of two thousand Madonna subjects, and to the Librarian of Congress for permission to use some of the Bolton Collection reproductions in this book.

DAVID T. O'DWYER.

FROM THE PRESSES OF
EASTERN OFFSET, INC
BALTIMORE, MD.